THE SpeakUp! METHOD OF Language Learning

SEAN YOUNG

Copyright © 2024 Sean Young
All rights reserved
First Edition

PAGE PUBLISHING
Conneaut Lake, PA

First originally published by Page Publishing 2024

ISBN 979-8-89315-725-3 (pbk)
ISBN 979-8-89315-749-9 (digital)

Printed in the United States of America

To Carmen Carneiro: I probably would not have gotten to where I am today without her. *Gracias, querida amiga. Tú eres una toda dar.*

And Dieter Schwarzbauer, my German teacher, who strengthened my love for languages even more.

For those exchange students who inspired me and kept my love for languages going, thank you, obrigado, gracias, kiitos, tack, and þakka þér fyrir. You all are still great friends to me.

Adriana Rezende (Brazil)
Camila Ferreira (Brazil)
Gabriela Contreras (Mexico)
Heili Sirkiä (Finland)
Johanna Arne (Sweden)
Kjarton Valdemarsson (Iceland)
Magnus Fabiansson (Sweden)
Minna Hakalin (Finland)

CONTENTS

Introduction vii
    The Speak Up! Method of Language Learning vii
    The Rosetta Stone Challenge x
    Speak Up! Languages x

The Rosetta Stone Challenge 1
    The Classroom Is Not the Real World 1
    Start with a Phrasebook 2
    Finding the Right Textbook 3
    Grammar References 7
    Newspapers and Radio 7
    Video and Movies 8
    Apps and Mobile Learning 9

Helping You Talk to the World 10
    Don't Believe the Hype 10
    Keeping It Real 12
    Do You Have the Time to Learn? 14
    Learning Pronunciation 15
    Learn by Using Dialogues 16
    Learn by Using Audio 18
    Learn with Grammar 18
    Do Your Exercises 19
    Learning Vocabulary 20
    Keep Practicing 22

A Teacher's Guide to Teaching Languages 26
    1.   The Teaching Environment 26
            Student-Centered Teaching 27
            Learning from Study 28
            Teacher Hints 29
            Let the Students Teach Themselves 30
    2.   Communication Strategies 31
            Listening Strategies 31
            Learning on the Spot 31

       Speaking Strategies 32
       Teach Ways to Control Conversations 33
       Word Whiskers 34
       Reading Strategies 36
       Writing Strategies 37
  3. What Should Be Taught? 38
       Teaching a Basic Foundation 38
       The Formalities 38
       Teaching Adjectives 39
       Elementary Verb Knowledge 40
       Focus on Meaning..46

The Power of Language 48
  Learning Without a Textbook..48
  The Power Chart Method 51
  Question and Answer Method...62
  Newspapers and Other Media 66

Learning with Artificial Intelligence 68
  The Impact of AI on Language Learning..............................68
  Personalized Learning...68
  Enhanced and Immediate Feedback 68
  The Downside of Using AI..69
  Privacy and Ethics 70

INTRODUCTION

The Speak Up! Method of Language Learning

I was twelve years old in early 1978 when I learned about the Rosetta Stone in school. Looking at the ancient Egyptian hieroglyphs fascinated me. And the more I read about that stone, the more I wanted to learn about that ancient language. But, of course, it wasn't easy since the only book I could find at the local library was *Easy Lessons in Egyptian Hieroglyphics* by Sir E.A. Wallis Budge. Even then, it wasn't easy using that book (as time went on, I made handwritten corrections in that book, much to the librarian's chagrin). But I did read all the books I could find about ancient Egyptian life, culture, etc.

1978–1982

I spent about two years learning ancient Egyptian when I moved on to ancient Greek and Hebrew. This time I was going to the reference books section of the local library to find what I needed, so there were more materials I could use to help me learn. The books there were quite academic and difficult to follow for a beginner. But learning a little bit of modern Greek and Hebrew helped a little bit.

1982

In 1982, with some knowledge of three ancient languages and two modern ones, I started attending German classes in school. And I *loved* it! Finally, a way to learn a language with actual feedback as to my progress. Vielen Dank, Herr Schwarzbauer!

In that class, there was an exchange student from Finland, and that got me thinking, *What does the Finnish language look like?* The only book I could find at the city library was a dictionary and a few books written entirely in Finnish. So...here goes nothing—I'm going to learn Finnish while also attending German classes.

When she saw that I was carrying a Finnish dictionary with me, she got all excited, checked out the dictionary, and wrote me a note: "You have to start studying Finnish [sic]—I'm going to test you!" So with her help, that dictionary, and a book written in Finnish, I was learning Finnish—language number seven.

1982–1985

Throughout the rest of my school years, I got to know the other exchange students and started checking out their languages. I met students from Sweden, Iceland, Germany, Brazil, Japan, and Mexico. Of course, I had to see what their languages were all about, right?

In November 1983. I met Carmen Carneiro, an exchange student from Mexico, who unknowingly gave me a boost in finding a way to simplify language learning. Because of a little bit of what I learned in the previous years, she helped me with some questions I had about the Spanish language. She was very patient and kind in this regard.

In June 1984, a couple of weeks before she returned to Mexico, we talked about the Portuguese language. I told her about the account of a French and Portuguese soldier talking about the spelling similarities in the French and Portuguese languages in the book *Native Tongues* (see below). She thought that was interesting and wondered what similarities could be found between Spanish and English. There were a few examples we thought up, and that sparked something in my brain: how many similarities are there between English, Spanish, and Portuguese?

Because of my previous experience with learning ancient Egyptian hieroglyphs and learning about the Rosetta Stone in school, I started researching the Spanish and Portuguese languages for ways to learn them quicker and easier than the language courses available at that time. My first breakthrough was in the book *Native Tongues* by Charles Berlitz:

> André Maurois has recounted an incident between soldiers who met in the trenches during WWI. A Portuguese soldier offered to teach a French soldier a thousand Portuguese words in less than one minute for one hundred francs. The French soldier accepted. "Look," said the Portuguese, all the words you have in French that end in -tion are the same in Portuguese, except that they end in -ção…there are over a thousand of them, and they are all feminine gender, just like French. That took less than a minute, didn't it? One hundred francs, please.

Because of that one paragraph, I decided to research languages—not the books, not the teaching methods, or scientific studies, but the languages themselves. I wanted to know what would make vocabulary and grammar easier to learn and retain in memory without all the headaches. I researched it for a couple of months before I came upon a book titled *The Mother Tongue* by Lancelot Hogben.[1] Through the use of examples from twelve European languages, that book helped me realize just how much languages have in common.

That's it! Starting with a fresh mind and outlook, I quit all knowledge and theories from the previous years on language learning and looked at just the languages themselves and what they have in common with not just English but also each other. As time went on, I was able to expand my list to a total of eleven European languages and a handful of other non-European languages.

[1] *Currently out of print. But you can still purchase a copy on Amazon.*

The Rosetta Stone Challenge

Now that I was finding these similarities and applying them to a language lesson format, I thought about what to name this method. Well, since the Rosetta Stone was what kicked things off, I called it *The Rosetta Stone Challenge,* and in the summer of 1984, I started putting it to use teaching Spanish and Portuguese. Eventually, I was able to apply the method to other languages, until by 1993, there were over twenty languages available.

Author's Note: The name and method of language learning in The Rosetta Stone Challenge are in no way affiliated with the Rosetta Stone language software. The Rosetta Stone Challenge is an original language course offered since June 1984 and is guaranteed to help you achieve conversational fluency within six to nine months.

Speak Up! Languages

In 1993, I decided to update the method to go along with changes in the way languages were evolving (current slang and idioms, spelling reforms, etc.). With another three years of development and testing, I was able to simplify the method a little more and add the ability to apply it to any language.

In 2004, I built a website to teach languages using the Speak Up! Method for people around the world to reach conversational fluency in their target language. In 2021, I retired from language teaching and am now working as an educational consultant. This book, along with the companion website, will give you the information you need to not just choose the right path to language learning but also achieve your goal of mastering a language.

▪ THE ROSETTA STONE CHALLENGE

The Classroom Is Not the Real World

You've started learning a new language. You're memorizing new words, making good use of flashcards, and you even go through the hard work of conjugating verbs and studying new grammar topics. That's okay, because the moment you've been waiting for has finally arrived: you meet a native speaker. You feel the excitement of getting ready to use what you've learned. You open your mouth to speak, "To greet you, my potato is John."

If you're studying a foreign language or have studied one in the past, then you know how difficult it is in the beginning to hold a conversation—much less start one. Reading, listening, and studying vocabulary and grammar is one thing, but when it comes time to go out to the real world and talk to others, it's like a whole different world.

When you decide to learn a new language, you may have questions about where to begin. Many people ask for recommendations on Facebook, Reddit, or Quora, seeking advice on what to study, how to learn, and which resources to use. However, the abundance of comments with different opinions and suggestions can be overwhelming and discourage you from pursuing your language learning goals.

As someone who has also commented on such threads, I understand the struggle. I've been learning languages since 1978, and I've been through frustrations and headaches. So, in response, I'm going to start you off with a trick that I learned very early in my language career.

Start with a Phrasebook

Although phrasebooks are mainly designed for travel purposes, they are still a helpful tool for your language learning needs. They contain simple words and phrases that are useful for basic communication. A mini-dictionary at the end of the book can help you build up your vocabulary, and some phrasebooks include a section dedicated to simple grammar rules, which can help you communicate more properly.

Back in 1993, I was offered a teaching job at the Lviv Polytechnic National University in Ukraine. At that time, the only knowledge I had of any Slavic languages was Czech, Polish, and Russian. At first glance, Ukrainian may look like Russian since they share the same Cyrillic alphabet, and I could read most materials and signage written in Ukrainian. Still, it's the spoken language that made it different enough that I had a slight struggle to understand much of what was being said around me.

Before entering Ukraine, I made sure to have an English-Ukrainian phrasebook with me for quick and easy communication. After settling into my apartment, I looked for a shop that sells small pocket-sized notebooks. And I would then turn it into my personal dictionary and phrasebook. Every time I heard a new word or phrase that sounded like it would be useful, I wrote it down in my notebook. Later in the evening, I would go over the new vocabulary and phrases and learn how to say them and when they could be used in conversation. By applying the Power Chart method in my language course, I was able to get conversationally fluent in Ukrainian within four months.

Even if you cannot travel to another country, by creating your own personal dictionary and phrasebook, you can build up useful vocabulary and phrases personalized to your needs. It's a way to organize the most practical information from your studies in one place for future use and to focus on things that you will need when speaking—all in one easy-to-carry location.

Another advantage to creating a personal phrasebook is that the process of writing these words and phrases down helps you memorize them. Even if you don't know how to write the alphabet or characters, at least write them as you hear them pronounced. It's a great tool for anyone studying any language at any level.

Finding the Right Textbook

There are thousands of books available in the language learning market that try to entice you to purchase them. However, don't be deceived by their attractive covers and the use of luring vocabulary that may convince you that you can become fluent in weeks or months. The truth is, no matter what they say to try and convince you of all that time and hard work to become fluent, you become fluent from the time you speak your first word or phrase.

Fluent, conversational, or both?

Whenever I ask a student what their language goals are, their usual response is, "I want to be fluent in (language)." Being fluent means speaking perfectly like a native speaker, right? What very few learners realize is that the common misconception of "being fluent" or "achieving fluency" is quite unrealistic and vague.

Very few people even speak their native language perfectly. And it's hard to define what it means to "speak like a native speaker" or to "speak perfectly." If you search an online dictionary for the term "fluent," you will come across the following definitions:

1. Spoken or written with ease:
2. Able to speak or write smoothly, easily, or readily:
3. Easy; graceful:
4. Flowing as a stream.
5. Capable of flowing; fluid, as liquids or gases.
6. Easily changed or adapted; pliant.

Did you see that the definitions of fluency do not specify a certain number of words to memorize or how much grammar you're supposed to perfect, or even set an amount of time to learn a language? It's important to be cautious of any language courses or books that claim to make you fluent in just a few weeks or months.

Take a moment to stop and think about what we want, and what we want is to be able to use the new language comfortably and without hesitation.

"Comfortably and without hesitation"—that is the way to describe fluency in another language.

But to be comfortable and use the language without hesitation in conversation is a matter of practicing what you do know and using that knowledge to talk around things that you don't know.

Being fluent in conversation is a matter of being comfortable with the language without constantly searching for words or hesitating when speaking. Don't let your insecurity get in the way of your skills. Focus on the words, phrases, and skills that are practical and useful to you in your daily interactions and practice them until you can master them.

What to look for in a language course

When you decide to look for a language course, be sure to find the best you can get. Take your time looking around; don't buy the first one you see or the one that claims to work miracles for someone else. You are not them. So what do you need to look for?

First things first

When looking for a book, it's important to check the original date of publication and any dates showing revisions. Avoid books published before 1960, as they tend to be too theoretical and academic. Textbooks from the 1970s through the 1990s have less academic style writing but still contain more information than is necessary. And with some languages (German, Norwegian, etc.), changes in spelling reform need to be considered.

The Speak Up! Method of Language Learning

Pronunciation notes

Most books will devote a few pages or an entire chapter to pronunciation that compares foreign sounds with those in your native tongue. Older books may give a letter in a foreign script, and the pronunciation part says "No English equivalent," with no attempt made to give you an idea of how to say it. Books that try to make it easier for the student to use symbols of the International Phonetic Alphabet to describe a certain sound (like an Arabic letter described as a voiced pharyngeal trill and pronounced like ʕ) can be discouraging. If audio examples of the sounds are available either on CD or MP3 format, listen to them instead and try to do the best you can.

How much information should be presented?

When selecting a language learning resource, it is important to consider the length of the lessons or chapters. Ideally, a lesson should be around three pages (six sides) long. If a lesson is longer than that, it may mean that the author is including too many unnecessary grammar explanations or spending too much time on exceptions and irregularities.

Look for a book where each lesson has a reading passage, a brief discussion of any new grammar concepts introduced in the reading, exercises based on the reading, and new vocabulary and phrases found in the lesson.

Grammar explanations

Each lesson should provide clear and concise grammar explanations for one or two major points covered in the current lesson. If needed, a couple of minor supporting points may be included as well, without overwhelming the learner. It's important to check if the grammar rules are explained well enough for the reader to understand on the first read or if they need to go through them multiple times. A good sign of a well-explained grammar rule is the use of clear examples and illustrations, along with vocabulary from current and past lessons.

Take note: If you come across tables and charts displaying various forms of a noun or verb and the text instructs you to memorize them, this could be a sign of a lazy author. Such authors are simply pushing their workload onto you. In such cases, it is better to look for another book.

Vocabulary lists

It is best to present vocabulary lists at the end of a lesson, after the exercises have been completed. To make it less overwhelming, only about twenty new words and phrases should be included, focusing on those introduced in the reading texts or grammar notes.

For the back-of-book vocabulary, there should be an instance of every new word from the lesson text in an English-Foreign and Foreign-English format. While keeping space limitations in mind, foreign words should have some indication of gender, such as noun declensions, verb conjugations, etc. This will help you understand how to properly use that particular word in conversation.

Reading texts

The purpose of a reading text is to demonstrate how language is used in a real-life setting without focusing too heavily on grammar and vocabulary. In the early stages of learning, the texts should be based on simple vocabulary and constructions, with gradual expansion as the course progresses. Another useful feature would be to include exercises related to the text after each passage, such as a Q and A. This helps gauge the progress of your comprehension skills.

Most textbooks avoid the use of reading passages as the primary learning material. Some introduce them later in the course, while others include them as supplemental material at the back of the book. This approach may indicate that the author is not proficient in writing a simple text using the fundamentals of the language, which may reflect a lack of knowledge in language teaching.

Quizzes and exercises

In the sections with exercises, look for those using complete sentences or maybe have a short reading passage. The sentences should contain at least one verb, a grammar point, and vocabulary from the lesson. It's important to cover most, if not all, of the grammar and vocabulary covered in the lesson. The exercises don't need to be complicated, but they should make sense.

You can use these exercises to check your work. Complete the exercises as shown in the lesson, and then try translating them back to the original language to see how accurate your work is.

Grammar References

A grammar reference is like a guidebook to the structure and theoretical knowledge of a language, just like blueprints are to a building. In its traditional form, each part of speech has its own section (noun, pronoun, adjective, verb, preposition, etc.). Each section has charts and tables showing the variations of these parts of speech and whether they follow a regular or irregular pattern.

Most reference grammar books provide examples of how each grammar point is used, while some have mini-exercises to help you learn better. However, keep in mind that they are not intended to be a complete learning book, as they lack structure and practical exercises to aid you in learning.

Be cautious of course books or materials that are heavily based on grammar reference style, with exercises that have very little to do with conversational ability. Treat it like a dictionary; use it when you need to clarify something for better understanding.

Newspapers and Radio

Newspapers are a great way to see how native speakers use the language. They usually cater to the home market and may be written in more casual or nonstandard speech forms. If you come across a section with comic strips or jokes, you've hit a gold mine! Absorb as much as you can from them. Write down any words or phrases you want to look up later. Try to incorporate them into your conversations, but make sure you're not being offensive or insulting. And don't hesitate to keep going back to these ever-constant sources of learning.

Radio and podcasts are similar to newspapers, but more for listening purposes. You may not understand much, if anything, at all in the beginning, since you'll be listening to fast and fluid speech intended for native audiences. But don't let that discourage you. Listen to the rhythm and flow of the speech.

It's important to keep in mind that some sounds may not be clearly reproduced by a physical speaker, such as in your car, on your mobile device, or on a handheld radio. This is particularly true with the sounds s, z, sh, f, v, th, etc. You don't notice these problems in your native language since the brain is used to hearing these imperfections and correcting them for you, so you can understand what is being said.

Digital recordings may help in making these sounds clearer, but they still make listening a challenging exercise. However, don't give up. The more you listen to them, the faster you will hear and understand the language, compared to just reading.

Video and Movies

Watching foreign-language movies can be an exciting way to immerse yourself in the language. Although you may find the speech too fast or colloquial at first, don't let that discourage you from watching. Pay attention to the actions, gestures, tone of voice, or background music, as they can help you follow the dialogue.

Streaming a movie or video on your device? Why not turn on the captions or subtitles while watching Netflix, Amazon Prime, Hulu, etc.? You can do the same with your DVD or Blu-ray player at home. YouTube has the option to turn on captions. This can be helpful in some cases, as you can pause the video and rewind if you didn't quite catch what was said. Keep in mind that some translated dialogues may not match what you've learned or heard before, so don't panic; write it down as best as you can and come back to it later.

It's recommended to watch these types of videos even when you're in the beginning stages of learning a language. Just relax and don't focus on translating anything at first. This allows the language to flow and helps improve your listening skills. Believe it or not, it will also help improve your speaking skills a lot.

Apps and Mobile Learning

The most significant change in language learning in recent years is the flood of apps for mobile devices. These in themselves are not methods but, rather, a different outlook on the presentation of materials. Learning with an app is mainly based on learning principles and rules that can also be found in the context of a textbook environment.

An app comes packaged in many different styles, colors, and various features to keep you active with your learning progress. If you take away all those colors, animations, and other features' you'll see they all pretty much do the same thing: they let you practice a sentence either through listening and repeating, filling in the blank, or comparing the target language with your native language. Vocabulary is learned through a popular flashcard format or matching-type game.

Getting through the app flows by playing a game, filling in a blank with a translation, or matching a correct translation to get the points you need to advance to the next level.

What you're doing is practicing logic and translation by observing and using the process of elimination to achieve a correct translation, and not much more. Doing this makes it seem like you're learning, when in reality, most of it may be forgotten within a couple of hours. You need to acquire an awareness of the flow and rhythm of a language to improve your ability to think in a new language, something apps do not provide.

▪ HELPING YOU TALK TO THE WORLD

Don't Believe the Hype

If you plan to learn a new language, it is essential to be cautious of unrealistic advertising strategies. Practically all language learning courses, methods, or books will promise you faster and easier results than what is achievable. Many people fail to learn a new language because they underestimate the effort required to learn it. Here are some common unrealistic expectations about language learning that you should avoid:

Myth number 1: You will be fluent in a matter of a few weeks or months.

Earlier in this book, we looked at the definition of the word fluent, what it means, and how you can achieve it with just one sentence. However, it is important to recognize that mastering a language or memorizing all of the vocabulary the traditional way is not possible. Learning a language, like any other skill, takes time and effort. Some people are naturally skilled with languages, while others excel in areas such as math, science, or music. Everyone has the potential to learn a language, but some individuals may have a greater aptitude for it than others.

Myth number 2: It will be very easy to learn. You saw smiling faces on TV and the website when you bought that language learning software; they were having the easiest time in the world. And the company's website said it was the fastest and easiest way to learn a language.

In my years of teaching and learning languages, I've met many people who were enthusiastic about learning a new language. They would go to the company's website or Amazon and buy one or two language course books, CDs, software packages, videos, and dictionaries, spending anywhere from $100 to $1,000 on language learning materials. Most of these people have been convinced to buy these courses because they look easy on TV and in the online ads. The reality is that most of these people may not be able to make it past the first few lessons, and their initial excitement will fade away now that they have hundreds of dollars' worth of language course materials that they will end up selling at their next garage sale for $20.

Myth number 3: Skip the exercises. Who needs to do exercises? You already sat through the lesson, and they expect you to do extra? Just move on to the next lesson or end your session early. You will remember all the topics later, when needed.

Exercises and practice quizzes in a language course are designed to allow you to practice the vocabulary and structure and to test yourself on how well you've learned or are learning in each lesson. They are not extra tasks that you can just skip by. When choosing a language course, look for one that has practice exercises scattered throughout the lesson, not just a set of ten to fifteen questions at the end of each lesson. These additional exercises can help reinforce what you're learning before moving on to the next section.

Myth number 4: Don't allow yourself to make mistakes. Mistakes are for losers. You're a winner. You must get everything right the first time you try it. Why subject yourself to the humiliation of making mistakes?

We all make mistakes, even in our native language. One of the biggest challenges for language learners is overcoming their fear of making mistakes. Some people may tell you that you'll be ridiculed or get into trouble if you say something wrong, but this may not be entirely true. Making mistakes is a natural part of the learning process. You need to practice to learn, and the more you practice, the fewer mistakes you will make. Don't be shy to use the language you are learning, because the more you speak, the better you will become at expressing yourself. So don't be afraid to make mistakes; keep practicing, and you'll be conversationally fluent in no time!

Myth number 5: Leave the language learning on the computer. You already spend an hour a day learning from your app or language software. That's too much already. So don't bother reviewing your notes or playing with flashcards later—they're not necessary. You learned it in the lessons, so why go further?

The human brain is lazy. It won't learn anything the first or second time something is being done. It's like a muscle; if you want it to grow stronger, you need to exercise it regularly. Similarly, to store information in your long-term memory, you need to repeat it regularly. This is why exercises and practice quizzes are important. They reinforce what you're learning in your permanent memory.

Don't just rely solely on your app or computer to learn a language. Take something with you to practice, such as flashcards, a notebook, or an MP3 player. A vocabulary and phrases trainer on my website can also help you practice on the go. These tools will help you use the language in real situations outside the classroom or at home. Try to find language opportunities around you (most packaged items in Europe and the United States are printed in multiple languages).

Now, let's explore some realistic approaches when it comes to learning a new language.

Keeping It Real

- Make a regular commitment. To learn a new language quickly and easily, it's important to make a regular commitment and dedicate time to it. Consistent exposure to the language is key, as the longer you wait between lessons, the more you'll forget. There are plenty of opportunities available to learn, practice, and review your language skills, so don't hesitate to take advantage of them. Remember that

The Speak Up! Method of Language Learning

repetition is essential when it comes to learning a language, so don't be afraid to revisit the material multiple times.
- Don't be shy. Learning a language will eventually involve using it, and that involves making mistakes in the beginning. Don't be afraid of sounding strange, awkward, or silly. If you don't open your mouth and speak, you'll miss out on making new friends or getting the information you need, especially in an emergency. You will impress people with your attempts at using the language.
- Proceed at your own pace. Don't feel pressured into thinking you have only one chance to learn information before moving on to new material. Read and listen to lessons or parts of lessons as many times as it takes to make you feel comfortable with what you're learning. You have all the time you need to learn. If you rush through, you make less progress.
- Take notes. Use a notebook and start a language journal. You'll learn much more quickly and effectively if you write it down or rephrase it in your own words once you've understood it. Include any vocabulary, grammar, practice examples, phrases from dialogues, and more. Take your notes with you to review whenever you have extra time, such as waiting for a bus or train at the airport, while dinner is cooking, etc.
- Don't worry about pronunciation. Listen to your audio several times. Listening is very important; you can't reproduce the sound until you hear and mimic it. Don't be afraid of sounding strange or being laughed at. Many celebrities, scientists, politicians, etc., speak English with a foreign accent and still communicate effectively. Just practice, and don't worry about 100 percent perfection.
- Go ahead and make mistakes. The more you speak and interact, the faster your mistakes will go away. So jump in and start talking! If you find you're making many errors, take things more slowly and practice the parts that are giving you trouble. Even when you speak to a native speaker

and he or she smiles at your performance, remember that it is usually a friendly smile, and they admire you for your effort as well as for what you have already achieved in their language. Native speakers generally focus their attention on the content of your message and not on how you should speak correctly. Look at errors as part of your learning process, and do not let them discourage you from practicing. Without practice, you cannot be successful.

Do You Have the Time to Learn?

Do not feel pressured to study for hours on end. Instead, aim to study for twenty to thirty minutes each day. Consistency is key, so try to make it a daily habit. If that's not possible, plan to study two to three times a week to keep your study routine going. Try to study around the same time each day, such as when you wake up, during lunchtime, or before bed. This will help you get into the habit of studying regularly. And, whenever you have some spare time, take a moment to refresh your memory.

Busy schedule?

Learning a new language can be challenging, especially when you have a busy schedule with work, school, or taking care of your children. However, I can relate to this struggle since I had a limited amount of time to learn a language as well. Nevertheless, I found ways to utilize my free time and make the most of it.

One of the significant time wasters in our daily routine is driving. We spend a considerable amount of time driving to work, back home, or running errands. This is an ideal opportunity to review your language skills by listening to a CD or MP3 player, a language podcast, or music. But I do want to emphasize that you must put safe driving practices first.

You can also use your waiting time to review your language skills. This could be while waiting in line at the grocery store, motor vehicle office, doctor's office, or bus stop. Carrying a notebook with you and reviewing the content you have learned or listening to audio files on your MP3 player or flashcards can help keep your mind fresh with the materials you are learning.

The best time to review?

A good time to review your study material is just before going to bed. Once you've brushed your teeth, changed into your pajamas, and gotten into bed, take some time to look over your lesson or notebook. Read it through slowly and carefully without trying to learn anything new. Allow your brain to process the information during the night, and it will transfer it into your permanent memory. The following day, you'll notice that you remember more of the material and have a better understanding of the lesson upon reviewing it the next day.

Learning Pronunciation

Pronouncing words accurately in a language can be intimidating, but it's not as daunting as it seems. Although there can be some sounds that appear difficult to make, with a little extra practice, they can be mastered in no time. The sounds for the letters B, D, K, L, M, N, P, Q, R, and T are pronounced almost identically in most languages and won't take much time or effort to reproduce.

Pause and rewind

It's important to take your time when practicing pronunciation. Don't let the recording get ahead of you. Make use of the pause and rewind buttons as much as you need to listen to the sounds of the word or phrase you're trying to learn. Listen as many times as necessary until you feel confident in your ability to say the word or phrase aloud.

If you find certain sounds difficult, spend extra time practicing them until you can pronounce them as correctly as possible. As you work through your language lessons, you'll find that these sounds will become easier to make.

If you come across words with unique pronunciation rules (such as the *ough* combination in English words like *rough*, *through*, *trough*, *bough*, and *cough*), be sure to take note of them in your notebook. Practice these words, paying attention to the spelling and the sounds needed to make them work for you. You can always revisit them later if needed.

Go out and speak!

To improve your language skills, it's important to use the language at every opportunity. You can try to meet someone who speaks the language you're learning or join a class to practice speaking with others. The more you speak the language, the better you'll become. You can also listen to native speakers to get a better idea of how the language is spoken. You can do this by listening to the radio, streaming a movie, watching YouTube videos, or downloading podcasts to see how much you can understand and to improve your pronunciation.

Learn by Using Dialogues

Most language courses and methods feature dialogues and conversations to demonstrate how the language is used in real-life situations. These dialogues are often designed to be realistic and relevant to the lesson at hand.

Before you start a lesson, it's recommended that you look through the dialogue to get an overall understanding of the conversation. Don't try learning or memorizing anything at this point. Instead, read through the dialogue a few times to grasp the main idea and see if you can comprehend the topic of the conversation.

Next, go back over the dialogue and focus on individual sentences. Are there any new words or grammar constructions you haven't encountered yet? If so, write them down in your notebook. You can also test yourself by attempting to figure out the meanings of the sentences or phrases just by looking at the context. This is a crucial skill that you'll need in real-life conversations, so it's essential to develop it as early as possible.

Once you've finished going over the dialogue, read through it again from start to finish. How much of it do you understand now? This exercise will help you gauge your progress and identify areas where you need to focus more attention.

For language courses with audio CDs or MP3

If you have purchased a language course that includes an audio package, it is recommended that you listen to the dialogues without repeating them. Listen as many times as you need to help improve your listening comprehension. Try to hear the sounds and pronunciation of the words, and note the sentence rhythm. Pay attention to where the speaker pauses at a comma or completes a sentence.

Next, listen to the audio from the beginning while following along with the text in your book. This will help you understand the dialogue better. By now, you should be familiar with most of the dialogue, and any new vocabulary words may become more recognizable. Try to write a summary of the dialogue in your notebook, noting details such as who is speaking, where they are, and what they are talking about.

What if your language course did not include any audio?

If your language course does not include any audio, do not worry. Work closely with the pronunciation section of the book and take your time to learn how to pronounce the sounds of the language accurately. There is no need to rush through the process. Get together with a native speaker or with your language partner to practice. When you eventually do get to the dialogue, cover a part of the dialogue or sentence and concentrate on a small bit at a time.

Learn by Using Audio

Learning a new language can be challenging, but using audio can be a great way to improve your skills. By listening to native speakers, you can hear how words are pronounced and how they are used in conversation. Listening is an essential skill that will help you understand what is being said around you.

When using audio during your lessons, focus on the specific parts that you need to learn at that time. For example, if you want to learn vocabulary words, you can isolate just the vocabulary list and listen to it multiple times. You don't have to listen to the entire lesson's audio all at once.

In addition to listening to the audio, there are other ways to use it effectively. You can read along with the words, sentences, or phrases while listening to the audio. You can also listen to audio from previous lessons as a review. Another option is to put the audio on an MP3 player and practice listening anywhere, anytime. Use the recordings as much as possible to improve your language skills.

Learn with Grammar

All languages follow certain patterns. These patterns are the nuts and bolts of the language—the rules that bind it together. Paying attention to grammar notes in lessons can help you learn the language more effectively. However, sometimes these notes may be long, confusing, and dull. Therefore, it is necessary to take a small section of grammar notes, read through it slowly, and take notes on each section in your own words. If needed, copy down any examples to show the grammar point in question. This will help you understand the concepts better.

While you're reading and writing out these samples in your notebook, look closely at the samples and see how the grammar points work in the sentence. Look at the dialogues to see where the new grammar point is used and learn the context it's in. Make changes by using vocabulary from previous lessons to vary the examples and test yourself on what you've learned.

Grammar flashcards

Flashcards can also be used to memorize grammar notes and examples. Put the sample sentences on one side of the card and the grammar point on the other. Then figure out what grammar point the sentence contains or how you can make a new sentence with the grammar point on the card.

Grammar in the wild

You can also use a search engine to find examples of grammar in the real world. For example, if you're learning French, type in "Je préfère un apéritif" and see what you find. This is a great way to practice and learn new constructions and vocabulary usage.

Come back to it

Just like vocabulary, repetition and review are essential for mastering grammar. Always go back and review your notes, including any previous lessons. Even if you have completed half the course, it's a good idea to review what you already know until it becomes easier.

Do Your Exercises

When you come across the exercise section of your language course, don't just write out the answers as expected. Take the time to write out entire sentences to get your mind used to constructing new material. And don't limit yourself to just reading and writing the answers to the exercises; read them aloud so you can practice your speaking and pronunciation skills at the same time.

To further your learning skills, try substituting vocabulary or grammar constructions from previous lessons. Not only will this help you learn different ways to answer the same question, but it will also help you remember and retain the different constructions needed in a conversation.

Some exercises require audio to sharpen listening skills. Before you begin, make sure to listen to the audio a few times before answering to be sure you understand what is being said. Use the pause button and answer as best you can with what you know. You can modify your answer using previously learned vocabulary and grammar. In real life, one question can have multiple answers.

Conversations have no answer key

Try solving the problem first, the best you can. Don't immediately look at the answer key at the end of the chapter or the back of the book to see if you've made the correct choice. There are ways to work it out. First, see if you can answer with what you just learned. Look at the dialogue used in the lesson and see if you can find a similar pattern to what you need, and use that to answer the question. Your answer may not be exactly what the answer key provides, but if it's close, you're fine. Take your time to complete these exercises before moving on to the next section.

When you finish the exercises, you're not completely done with them. You can always go back and do them as many times as you want during your studies to revise and refresh your memory. It's important to practice what you've learned regularly.

Learning Vocabulary

Learning a new language involves acquiring new words and learning how to combine them into sentences. While memorizing new words might seem easy during lessons, it takes practice to make them stick in your long-term memory. Simply looking at a new word and repeating it a few times won't do the trick. You need to find a method or two that works best for you to help embed the new word into your memory. Experiment with different tactics until you find the one that works best for you. Here are some methods that you can try out to help you memorize new vocabulary.

Audio repetition

To improve your pronunciation and become familiar with the sounds of a native speaker, it's important to look at the written form of the word and listen to the audio multiple times. This may require frequent use of the pause and rewind buttons on your CD or MP3 player. This will help you to hear the pronunciation accurately and become accustomed to the native speaker's sounds.

Spoken repetition is a helpful learning method that can be used in two ways:

(1) You can practice along with the audio exercise provided above and try saying the word or phrase multiple times aloud. Listen carefully to how the speaker pronounces the word and repeat it. Then, without the audio, continue saying the word repeatedly until you can pronounce it easily. This exercise will not only help you hear the word as you speak it but also improve your speaking skills by training your tongue and mouth to get used to the new movements required to pronounce the word correctly.

(2) You can also try looking at the word letter-by-letter and see if you can pronounce it. It's important not to rush and try to say the word too quickly. Instead, repeat it slowly and naturally, focusing on pronouncing it as accurately as possible.

Written repetition

Take a sheet of paper and write the word as many times as you want until you can write it naturally. Start slowly and carefully, especially if you are learning a language that doesn't use a Latin-based alphabet or is written in the opposite direction of your native language (like Arabic, Hebrew, or even Chinese and Japanese!). As you write, say the word aloud to help your brain remember it. Fill up an entire page with vocabulary words to get your hands used to the new movements and to teach your brain these new words.

Flashcards

These are very effective for learning new words. If you don't want to buy index cards, cut some paper into small squares, about two inches by two inches. Write a new vocabulary word on one side and the English translation on the other side. Shuffle the cards and start going through them. Look at the foreign words, say them aloud, and give the English translation. You can also start with English and say what it is in your new language. Use the vocabulary words that are used in the lesson you are currently studying or carry a common theme.

On this book's companion website, you'll find vocabulary trainers that will help you learn words just as effectively as traditional flashcards.

A review is always good. Look for new vocabulary words in the dialogues and see how they are used. Copy those sentences in your learning notebook, and remember to look back at older vocabulary lists or example sentences and review them. Listen to the vocabulary audio and listen to it again.

Keep Practicing

Speakers of English know the old cliché: "Practice makes perfect," and it is very true in the world of language learning. Imagine this: you dedicate thirty minutes a day to studying Spanish, either online or through classroom course materials. What do you think will happen if you turn off your computer and stop learning for a whole week? Chances are, everything you learned the previous week will either be lost or you will be facing a lot of review time.

The human brain is lazy, and it doesn't like to retain anything new. Practicing and doing it often is the only way to get your brain to accept the fact that you want to put this stuff in there. And don't fall into the trap that if you have limited time to dedicate to language learning, it doesn't mean that you don't have time to practice your language.

Practice with a native speaker during a coffee break or lunch. Try to read any foreign language signs on the bus or in the shops when you're out and about. It also helps to talk to yourself in the language you're learning. Look around you and see if you can recall any vocabulary words for the things around you. There are so many "time wasters" out there that you can take advantage of to help strengthen your skills.

If you're looking to improve your speaking, try to practice speaking at least three times per week. Before you let this idea scare you, there are a few excellent ways to practice speaking:

Speaking with native speakers.

Most native speakers are almost always happy to help you learn their language, either online, over the phone, or in person. Remember, don't be shy! If you meet a native speaker of the language you're learning, go ahead and ask for help.

You will find thousands of native speakers in Facebook groups, or you can watch movies and videos on services like YouTube, Hulu, Netflix, etc. to keep your ears in tune.

Speaking with other learners.

When it comes to learning a language, you're not alone. If you're reading this book, you're no stranger to the Internet and all the resources it provides for learning new things and meeting new people. Search online for those who are learning the same language as you are and start a study group or set up weekly chats on Zoom, FaceTime, or Skype—even by phone is great too!

Meeting up and interacting with others learning the same language keeps learning easier and more fun. Your motivation stays high, and you have a perfect language partner who can teach you things you can't teach yourself.

Talking to yourself

What if you can't find someone or your language partner is not available at the moment? Don't skip practicing because you have yourself with whom to practice. How much time do you spend every day thinking and going through internal dialogues? This can become a wonderful opportunity simply by turning that internal dialogue into the language that you're learning. It will better prepare you for conversations with others.

Imitating speeches and songs.

If you want to speed up the pace of listening to and speaking a new language, go online or use one of the available streaming services to find a movie or a scene from a movie in the language that you're studying (if there isn't one, see if maybe the audio has the language available). First, watch it a couple of times to become familiar with it and take note of the context of the scene. Then, little by little, rewind and play the scene. Pause it so you can try to imitate what you're hearing. Once you're ready, repeat what the actor or speaker says, word for word. With practice and patience, you'll be speaking just like a native speaker, with all the rhythm and nuances of pronunciation, along with picking up new vocabulary and phrases. Again, write down any new stuff in your dictionary. The same can be done with songs, in which you can find the lyrics to them and sing along.

Practice with as many people as possible as much as possible. This way, you're adapting to the huge variety of dialects, accents, and speaking styles out there. Not only does this make it easier to understand just about any native speaker, but you will also be able to communicate with them like a native.

Record your conversations

I understand that very few people enjoy being recorded or filmed. The very thought of it makes most people uncomfortable. But recording yourself speaking another language helps you become less nervous when speaking.

What you do is use your phone, video camera, or any other recording device to allow yourself to review and find ways to improve your conversations. You can look up words that you couldn't remember during the conversation. Earlier, I spoke about fillers and connectors in talking—find ways to add them in. How can you improve your pronunciation? And other things you can find to polish up your conversational fluency.

Overall, learning a foreign language and becoming conversationally fluent is easier than you think, and all you need is to be confident in what you know and comfortable using it when speaking. There are many ways to improve your fluency and skills in your foreign language. With motivation, dedication, and plenty of practice, you'll be speaking fluently in no time!

▪ A TEACHER'S GUIDE TO TEACHING LANGUAGES

1. The Teaching Environment

The biggest flaw in every language learning environment is the antiquated methods of teaching. This is not the fault of the teacher. The fault lies in the belief that language must be learned as an academic exercise where the teacher uses most of the class time lecturing about grammar rules, making the student listen and repeat vocabulary, and spending little time on actual conversation. This is teaching them how to fail—again, not the fault of the teacher. I've seen students get very high marks in their classes, getting up to advanced lessons by their graduation. But once they're outside the classroom, they can barely get out a sentence to order a meal.

In the traditional teaching environment, learning is typically limited to a classroom setting. The teacher assumes the roles of both instructor and decision-maker, guiding students in their learning. The most common seating arrangement is to place desks in evenly spaced rows facing the teacher's desk. The lesson's content and delivery are considered to be the most important aspects, and students are expected to master knowledge through rote learning, drills, and practice.

During instruction, the teacher is constantly on the move, engaging students as a single entity. The teacher is responsible for making decisions about how or when instruction should take place. However, this method comes with its own set of challenges. Students tend to get bored easily, and their attention can quickly wander. This can cause delays in the lessons, creating frustration or annoyance among other students.

To successfully learn a language and make it stick, the student needs to think. They need to see the problem and, using any previous lesson material, logically find the solution they need. They may need to enlist the help of other students in the classroom. Of course, mistakes will be made in the beginning, but as the student continues to use the solution they came up with and refines it through use and practice, these mistakes eventually go away.

Fortunately, there is a way to overcome this problem and maximize the learning process. By giving more of the teaching responsibilities to the student, they can become more engaged and take an active role in their learning. This approach can help students stay focused and motivated, leading to a more effective learning experience.

In this section, you'll learn how to set up the classroom in a way that maximizes the student's learning capabilities and how you can help maximize the student's learning skills. I'll be using Spanish as a language example. On this book's companion website, you'll find examples using other popular languages.

Student-Centered Teaching

When you place the responsibility of learning on the students themselves, they become more invested in their education and are empowered to take control of their learning process. As they discover new knowledge and solutions, they can form their own conclusions and develop a deeper understanding of the material. However, this approach may not be effective in a traditional classroom setting. In my experience, the most effective student-centered learning environment is achieved through smaller, more manageable groups.

Group set-up

Organizing students into small groups is a more effective and personalized way to learn a language. To create an optimal learning environment, a classroom can be divided into circles of four to six students per group. This allows students to share knowledge, maintain eye contact, and access materials with minimal distractions from other groups.

Group management

Managing a group ensures that tasks are completed efficiently, especially when dealing with students who might have varying characteristics such as being gifted, socially challenged, disruptive, or unmotivated. It may be necessary to use different management techniques, depending on the situation.

You will also need to have a balanced mix of advanced and disruptive students in the group. This will provide diversity and help develop the social skills of all students. Additionally, it will support the growth of other students in the group.

To keep track of the group's progress, you can assign one of the students to observe the group's activities and report back to the teacher. The observer can identify areas where the group is struggling and suggest strategies that would assist the group.

Learning from Study

Once the students have been assigned to groups, distribute and introduce the lesson materials to each group. There's no need to teach them anything at this stage, as it's just a quick review to let them know what to expect. Allow them some time to go through the learning materials together with their group members and see how much they can learn on their own. Let them talk among themselves, correct one another, and ask or answer questions. When they encounter difficulties or the group collectively struggles to grasp a concept, guide them in identifying where they need to correct their mistakes or improve their findings without providing a solution.

When the students are outside the classroom, have them look for information in the language they are learning and read or learn as much as they can to the best of their abilities. If possible, ask them to bring the materials they have read or found to their assigned group and help each other with their findings or correct any mistakes. Materials can include browsing websites, purchasing a newspaper or magazine, or watching a DVD or TV program. Can something be shared among the groups? Encourage that too.

The Speak Up! Method of Language Learning

Teacher Hints

To maximize learning and get the most out of lessons, setting up the learning environment is crucial.

- Keep the classroom free of unnecessary distractions. Only the resources for the lesson currently being studied are ready to be accessed.
- Carefully consider the needs of the student, particularly ensuring that every student can see and hear from every part of the room and that there is plenty of space to move around.
- Always ensure you can make eye contact with all students in the class.
- Be aware of health and safety issues.
- Make materials and supplies easily accessible to prevent delays, disruptions, and confusion. Place frequently used materials in different places around the room.
- Learning can be more effective if students have the opportunity to move around, interact with other groups, and obtain information from them.
- If using posters or wall decorations, try to keep cultural diversity consistent within the classroom.

Once the learning environment is established, there are a variety of strategies to maintain the learning process:

- *Motivate their learning.* As much as possible, always hand out new material in the context of situations to which the students can relate in terms of their personal and career experiences, rather than simply as more material to memorize.
- *Make good use of visuals.* Use photographs, drawings, sketches, and cartoons to illustrate and reinforce the meanings of vocabulary words or lesson materials. Show

Spanish-language videos or TV shows to the students to see how Spanish is used in daily life.
- *Assign some basic exercises* to provide conversation practice for the vocabulary and grammar points learned in the lesson.
- *Keep in contact:* With the student's permission, see if you can get them together into a group chat with the app available in your country (WhatsApp, Telegram, Line, etc.) where they can keep in touch with each other, ask questions, and share new materials they've found or learned.

One more thing: avoid the temptation of filling every minute with lecturing and writing on the board. Give the students some time to process the information presented to them and discuss it with their peers. Encourage them to brainstorm ideas and solutions together. You can also introduce group activities, such as team competitions, to work on questions and problems.

Let the Students Teach Themselves

As a teacher, it's important to recognize that each student knows how they learn best and what problems they come upon and get around them. Allowing students to learn in a group environment can help them identify their weaknesses and work together with their peers to find the best solutions that suit their individual needs. Your role as a teacher is to provide instructional materials and monitor their progress, rather than dictating every step of the process. If a student or the group as a whole requires assistance, avoid providing them with the answer. Instead, use open-ended questions and reasoning to help them solve problems on their own. This approach can help build their confidence and independence in their studies.

2. Communication Strategies

Listening Strategies

What is the best way to learn a new language? Is it by speaking or listening? Listening plays a crucial role in language learning because if you can't hear the sounds of the new language, you won't be able to reproduce them. It takes time to comprehend and start using new words and expressions, and listening helps us achieve that.

Listening is not a passive skill. It requires active thinking, where we take the parts of the conversation that we understand and use guessing and context to understand the whole conversation. When we want to learn how to say something, we first listen to how others say it. Although it's helpful to ask for clarification or repetition, we try to remember how it was said so we can use it later if needed.

To help students improve their listening skills, here are a few things they can do: assign an audio recording as homework so they can actively learn outside the classroom. Alternatively, you can bring some recordings to class and distribute them to the groups. When listening to the recordings, get the students to work together in groups to help each other understand words and phrases that they have not yet learned or known.

To keep your lesson plans consistent, you don't have to use the radio. You can take a recording of a conversation, a newscast, music, or anything else. If you can obtain a transcript of the recording, that's even better. Let students follow along with the transcript to clear up any possible misunderstandings.

Learning on the Spot

At times, a student may have to engage in a personal conversation with a fellow student or a native speaker. This is when the student must be able to learn on the spot since they won't always have their textbooks, dictionaries, or even you around to assist them. Therefore, it is essential to teach the student how to listen selectively.

They should focus on listening to one item at a time, preferably in the given order:

1. Tone of voice
2. Similar sounds in English and the language
3. Sounds not found in English
4. Individual words or phrases
5. Grammatical forms

It's important to try to understand the meaning of what others are saying. Students can do this by looking for clues in keywords, gestures, intonation, and facial expressions. If possible, ask the student to repeat back what they think the speaker said and ask for confirmation. Watching movies without subtitles is also a good way to look at the mannerisms used to see what the person is talking about.

To improve listening skills, have the students listen to conversations whenever they can without being too obvious. Listen for words and phrases they already know, have them try to understand the overall meaning of the conversation, and observe non-verbal cues. You may also have your students listen to international radio to hear how the language sounds in real-world conversations. The best websites I've found for streaming radio are:

BBC (British Broadcasting Corporation): http://www.bbc.co.uk
VOA (Voice of America): http://www.voanews.com
Radio Stations: http://www.radio-locator.com

Speaking Strategies

If your student can listen to and understand a conversation but struggles to construct a sentence, don't get impatient. It's natural to understand more than what we can say during the beginning and intermediate stages of learning a language. Speaking skills are more complex than listening skills because they require the production of new sounds and structures. Encourage your students to listen carefully, as this will improve their understanding and speed up their speaking progress.

To communicate effectively, we need to express our thoughts and feelings, and we need the listener to understand them from our words and body language. To speak a language effectively, a student needs to make the sounds of the language flow as best they can in a way that can be understood. Contrary to popular belief, you don't have to speak perfectly to communicate with others. The goal is to put words, phrases, and sentences together in a way that can be understood by native speakers.

In addition to speaking correctly, it's essential to speak in a culturally acceptable way. This includes knowing how and when to begin a conversation, interrupt, ask for clarification, change the topic, and end the conversation.

Teach Ways to Control Conversations

When a student is learning a new language, they are often taught to give control of the conversation to the other person. Typically, they would say something, listen to the response, speak again, and continue like this, ad nauseam. However, to keep practicing speaking skills, it's useful to learn how to control the conversation.

The most basic strategy for controlling a conversation is to ask questions that require a "yes" or "no" answer. This helps the student practice speaking and also allows them to gauge whether the other person has understood. Other tips for controlling a conversation include:

- Keep the listener guessing so they do not know what may be said next. For example, when going shopping, let the student get what they want first, and then ask a question or two about things they have no intention of buying.
- When asking for a particular item, have the student hold or look at something else (the student holds a bag of apples but inquires about the freshness of the bananas or the price of a container of milk). If more than one of the same items is needed, practice the routine in several different shops.

This will allow the student to practice speaking as well as understanding different responses.
- Prepare a conversation starter in advance so the student is in control of at least the first topic you talk about, then strike up conversations on public transportation. If the student is afraid of getting into a long conversation, let them wait until they are close to their destination before starting a conversation.
- You can also pair up two students and give them a common topic to speak about. Let them sit in different places in a public place, strike up a conversation with someone, and then compare notes afterward.

Teach the students the various phrases used during conversation to ensure they have expressed themselves clearly.
"Did I say that right?"
"What would it mean if I said, ___?"
"Would you say, ___ to a man, a woman, a child, or someone older?"

Word Whiskers

In the beginning phases of learning, the student's slow speech causes their tongue to run and hide while their brain is trying to find the word or answer they need. This creates what is called "word whiskers" and usually comes out as *um*, *uh*, and *you know*. This part of language is important and useful in making conversation, even though it's seriously neglected in textbooks and language courses. Using Spanish word whiskers as an example: Quiero...*este*...*ir*...*o sea*...al cine *¿no?*

Filling in the conversation

To sound even more like a native speaker, teach the student how to fill in a conversation. When speaking our native language, our conversations have these seemingly insignificant filler words that help us connect ideas and fill in empty spaces. Learning these connectors contributes immensely to keeping us from sounding like textbook-reading parrots. Take a look at these commonly used fillers and see how many of them you use in your conversations:

- *Fillers*
    - Well...
    - actually...
    - so...
- *Elaborations*
    - More specifically...
    - in other words...
- *Openers*
    - That's a good question...
    - I was thinking...
    - So...
- *Closers*
    - Overall...
    - Basically, that's it...
    - In the end...
- *Apologies*
    - I'm sorry, but...
    - I've got to be honest with you...
- *(Dis)Agreement*
    - Definitely...
    - I completely agree...
    - I don't really agree...
- *Passing*
    - What about you?
    - What do you think?
- *Qualifiers*
    - To be honest...
    - To tell you the truth...
    - Actually...
    - In reality...

- *Quotes*
    - Recently, I heard that...
    - They say that...
- *Switches*
    - By the way...
    - Oh, I forgot to tell you...

Learning and using these connectors makes your student sound more native-like than they are and gives a boost to their confidence in speaking. There's no need to learn all of them in one sitting. Have the student pick out what's important to their needs and see about using it in conversation. Also, have your student write them in their personal phrasebook for future reference.

Reading Strategies

When students start reading, they may feel intimidated because they can't understand every word. However, they don't need to understand every single word or grammatical construction to get the main idea of what they are reading. To improve their reading skills, students need to develop the ability to read for overall meaning and specific information. Here are some simple strategies to help them out:

1. Before reading, have the students make guesses about the topic or main idea by looking at the title of the text and any accompanying pictures. Is there anything they might already know about the topic?
2. Read through the piece once without stopping to get a general idea of what the text is about. Allow students to skip over unfamiliar words or grammatical constructions in the initial reading.
3. After reading the text once, give them a few moments to reflect, and then ask them to read it again to see how much more they can understand.
4. Read it again, this time underlining only the words or grammatical constructions that keep them from under-

standing the main part of the text. Students can get help from others in the group if they are stuck.

Other ways students can improve their reading skills include practicing reading sentences from past lessons or writing in their journals. Reading excerpts from newspapers, magazines, and children's stories is also a great way to read the language "in the wild." Encourage them to make good use of headlines, pictures, and diagrams found between the pages.

Writing Strategies

When learning a new language, writing plays a crucial role in the process. It helps the student practice and improve their writing skills, spelling, and grammar. Writing also does wonders for memory; it allows the brain to retain information more efficiently than when just listening and repeating. Thus, it helps to develop other communication skills. Some ideas for effective writing practice include:

- Hand out selected texts from newspapers, magazines, and children's books, if available in the language being taught. While writing them, the student should focus on details such as spelling, word order, verb tenses, and other grammatical points.
- Always write the answers to any exercises in full. For instance, if it's a fill-in-the-blank exercise, the student should write the entire sentence with the correct answer instead of just writing the answer.
- Ask a member of the group to dictate parts of a newspaper article or sentence, and have the rest of the group write the text. Then, exchange papers with others in the group and check for mistakes. Rewrite the sentences that had errors.

In addition, you can take texts from previously learned lessons and let the students modify them with what they already know. For example, they can change the verb tenses, change singular to plural, summarize or paraphrase the text, etc.

3. What Should Be Taught?

Author's note: The examples shown in this section will be using the Spanish language. The same principles can be applied to any other language, whenever possible.

Teaching a Basic Foundation

When learning grammar in any language, there is no perfect way to start teaching or learning grammar. Factors such as the teaching methods, the language being learned, and the lesson materials can affect the learning process. I don't believe in teaching the stiff, formal language rules as traditionally taught in books and classes. Instead, I prefer to combine important grammar rules with the realities of the language needed to survive in a non-English environment. For beginner students, some basic grammar rules can be learned to provide them with a foundation to build upon when learning outside the classroom. By learning half of what they need to know, students can have a good foundation in any language.

The Formalities

Being formal is more than just knowing the formal parts of speech and being polite. Formalities include mannerisms, body language, and how you treat others in passing.

For instance, let's say a student is touring Madrid with a group of tourists. They decide to explore some off-the-beaten-path shops and cafes to put their Spanish language skills to the test. Depending on how confident they are in their language abilities, they may use Spanish wherever they go, or fear of using the language can cause them to use English, which could make them come across as either shy or arrogant. For example, if the student spends a lot of time browsing in a shop without saying a word or not acknowledging someone who greets them, it could give off the impression of rudeness.

It's essential to teach students that, in any foreign language environment, they should greet people whose space they have invaded, even if briefly. It isn't necessary to greet everyone they encounter, but acknowledging a shop clerk, waiter, secretary, or guest can help create a positive first impression and make new friends. Moreover, certain services may improve after greeting someone in their language.

It's also worth noting that most languages require more spoken formalities than English. Skipping over them may be perceived as rude.

Other formalities to keep in mind include shaking hands when meeting or leaving someone, engaging in small talk before getting down to business, and observing cultural norms.

Teaching Adjectives

One common mistake made by books and language courses is delaying the learning of adjectives in the initial stages of study. As a result, students struggle to describe objects or create awkward sentence structures until they reach the lesson on adjectives. For example, consider the following Spanish sentences:

How was the film? Muy, muy, muy buena

How was the meal? No, muy buena.

Constructions like these may sound strange to Spanish speakers. If your students have picked up these habits, teach them alternate ways to express themselves. Additionally, certain prefixes and suffixes can modify adjectives in Spanish, which can help your student expand their vocabulary quickly. Here are some examples:

muy
muy bueno, muy bien—very good, very well
e-/re-
elindo, retelindo—very pretty
muy re-
muy rebonito—very very pretty

re-/rete-
regrande, retegrande—very big
-ísimo; -ísima
Hábil, habilísimo—skillful, very skillful
querido, queridísimo—dear, very dear
diligente, diligentísimo—diligent, very diligent
pronto, prontísimo—soon, very soon
lejos, lejísimo—far, very far
cerca, cerquísima—near, very near
ricamente, riquísimamente—richly, very richly

It is highly beneficial for students to learn how to communicate effectively through conversation. Teaching them early on the use of suffixes and prefixes with adjectives can increase their vocabulary with minimal effort.

Elementary Verb Knowledge

Verbs and nouns are the two most important components of any language. Verbs provide the necessary details to convey what is happening, and they change their structure to indicate specifically who is doing what. This is the grammar section that most students dread due to the various forms of the verb that they must memorize. However, it is not as difficult as it may seem.

Learning every form of the verb—even the ones that are seldom used or not used at all—can be intimidating for a student. It can consume a significant amount of time and energy that could have been spent on learning the most important aspect of any language: communication. The best way to start a student's language learning journey is by focusing on the most essential verb forms:

Present tense

The present tense is a basic form of verb conjugation that corresponds to the English present tense. For instance, "Bailo" means "I dance" and "Estoy bailando" means "I am dancing." However,

The Speak Up! Method of Language Learning

the traditional method of learning the present tense of verbs can be overwhelming for students. The chart showing how to conjugate the verb in all persons may cause confusion or frustration and slow down the learning process.

Subject	*Estar*	*Hacer*	*Sentir*	*Conducir*
Yo	estoy	hago	siento	conduzco
Tú	estás	haces	sientes	conduces
Él	está	hace	siente	conduce
Ella	está	hace	siente	conduce
Usted	está	hace	siente	conduce
Nosotros / Nosotras	estamos	hacemos	sentimos	conducimos
Vosotros / Vosotras	estáis	hacéis	sentís	conducís
Ellos / Ellas	están	hacen	sienten	conducen
Ustedes	están	hacen	sienten	conducen

Instead, it is recommended to start with the most basic forms of the present tense. The student only needs to know how to drop the infinitive ending (in this case, -ar) and add -*o* to indicate I, -*as* for you (in an informal situation), or -*a* to indicate he, she, it, or you (in a formal situation). This way, the student can gradually learn the other forms of the present tense without feeling overwhelmed.

(yo) Tom<u>o</u> agua—<u>I</u> drink water/<u>I am</u> drink<u>ing</u> water

(tú) Tom<u>as</u> agua—<u>You</u> drink water/<u>You are</u> drink<u>ing</u> water

(Usted) Tom<u>a</u> agua—<u>You</u> drink water/<u>You are</u> drink<u>ing</u> water

(el, ella) Tom<u>a</u> agua—<u>He or She</u> drinks water/<u>He or She is</u> drink<u>ing</u> water

These three verb conjugations are the most frequently used in basic one-on-one conversations. Therefore, it is advisable to teach these forms first and focus on them in the beginning. The remaining conjugations can be covered at a later stage during their studies.

Past tense

Unlike English, Spanish has two simple past tenses: preterit and imperfect indicative. These tenses are not interchangeable. In general, the preterit is used when referring to a completed action, that is, when the verb refers to an action that has a definite end. On the other hand, the imperfect indicative is used to refer to an action that doesn't have a specific ending. The imperfect tense is so named because "imperfect" can also mean "incomplete."

Let's take a look at the differences here. The preterit is used:

1. To tell of something that happened once
    a. Fui ayer a la tienda.—I went to the store yesterday.
    b. Escribí la carta.—I wrote the letter.
2. To tell of something that happened more than once but with a specific end
    a. Fui ayer a la tienda seis veces.—I went to the store six times yesterday.
    b. Leyó el libro cinco veces.—He read the book five times.
3. To indicate the beginning or end of a process
    a. Tuvo frío.—He got cold.
    b. El huracán se terminó a las ocho.—The hurricane was over at eight.

The imperfect indicative is used:

1. To tell of past habitual or repeated actions
    a. Iba a la tienda.—I used to go to the store.
    b. Escribía muchas cartas.—I wrote many letters.
2. To describe a condition, mental state, or state of being from the past
    a. Había una casa aquí.—There used to be a house here.
    b. Tenía frío.—He was cold.
3. To describe an action that occurred over an unspecified time
    a. Lavaban las manos.—They were washing their hands.

4. To indicate time or age in the past
   a. Era la una de la tarde.—It was 1:00 p.m.
   b. Tenía 43 años.—She was forty-three years old.

There are differences between the two tenses, but I won't go into detail about them in this book. Some of the sentences above could be expressed in the other tense, which would change their meaning. For instance, while "escribía muchas cartas" would describe something that usually happened over an unspecified period, one could also say "escribí muchas cartas" to indicate a specific point in time.

Future tense

When it comes to talking about future plans in Spanish, there are many ways to express them. However, traditional teaching methods can often make these expressions sound formal or awkward. As a result, I encourage my students to take a more natural approach to speaking like a native speaker by simply ignoring these expressions altogether. Unlike in English, the present tense is commonly used in Spanish to indicate future actions. Therefore, it's easier for students to start speaking about their intentions or future plans with more fluency and confidence.:

Are you coming tomorrow?—¿Vienes mañana?
See you later—Nos vemos
I'll give it to you Tuesday—Te lo doy el martés

If you're worried that the future is not going to be understood, Spanish speakers listen to the context of the statement or question to determine how the future is expressed.

Te cuento—I'll tell you (now) as opposed to Te contaré—I'll tell you (someday)

Mañana te cuento—I'll tell you tomorrow and Mañana te contaré—I shall tell you tomorrow

Can you see the differences in the construction of those sentences? *Te cuento* is in the present tense, whereas *Te contaré* is in the perfectly conjugated future. With the addition of a time indicator (mañana), you can still express the future using just the present tense.

Therefore, *mañana te cuento* uses the present tense with a time indicator, while *te contaré* uses a future conjugated verb without indicating when the action will be performed. The traditional conjugated forms can be pretty much saved for very formal situations. Other time indicators the student can use are: *pasado mañana, la semana próxima, la semana siguiente, el mes (año) próximo, el mes (año) siguiente*

Using the power verb "ir"

The second way to express the future is by using the verb "ir" (to go). This is found in English under the guise of "going to do something."

Mañana voy a llamar—Tomorrow I'm going to call

La semana próxima voy al teatro—Next week I'm going to the theater.

This can also be used with or without a time indicator.

Power verbs

A power verb is a verb that can be used to form dozens (if not hundreds) of statements, questions, or commands. The structures are easy to form and will be grammatically correct. It has been a very popular concept with my students over the years, and it can be modified to whatever circumstances are needed.

Later in this book, under the section "The Power of Language," we'll get into more details as to what they are and how to use them.

On this book's companion website, you will find downloadable charts and online exercises to help you use Power Verbs and the charts for use in various situations (shopping, seeing the doctor, taking transportation, etc.) Downloadable worksheets can also be printed out for your students to use in their studies.

Shoe verbs

A verb with an irregular conjugation (also known as a show or boot verb) is a verb that has a consistent pattern of changes in the stem. The most common changes are those stems that have an -o- or -e-. Take a look at these examples:

-o- becomes -ue- : dormir—d*ue*rmo, d*ue*rmes, d*ue*rme, etc.

-e- becomes -ie- : querer—qu*ie*ro, qu*ie*res, qu*ie*re, etc.

If you put these types of verbs in chart form, you'll see that when a line is drawn around them, they form the shape of a shoe.

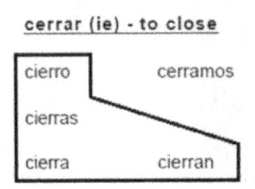

cerrar (ie) - to close

cierro	cerramos
cierras	
cierra	cierran

Here are some common shoe verbs to begin with:

o—ue verbs
probar—to try on, to test
mover—to move
dormir—to sleep
contar—to count, to tell
doler—to hurt
encontrar—to find
volver—to return

e—ie verbs
comenzar—to begin, start
empezar—to begin, start
entender—to understand
extender—to extend
nevar—to snow
pensar—to think, plan
perder—to lose
preferir—to prefer
querer—to want, wish, love
sentir—to feel
tener—to have
venir—to come

Focus on Meaning

As a teacher, you've heard about cognates, yet they are rarely used or touched on in language courses. Always use them to the fullest. Let the students find them and don't make them have to learn them (much like having to learn how to brush your teeth every night over and over again—it's a waste of time). Otherwise, vocabulary building can also be done through exercises such as:

1. Instead of giving the student the traditional "English=Language," try giving them paraphrases of word definitions in the text:
   journey—He went on a journey
   ate—I ate chicken and rice for dinner
2. Use multiple-choice items to find the correct definitions for words in the text:
   Monkey
   a. comical
   b. small
   c. precious
   d. serious
3. Give just the definitions of words in a text and have the student look for those words:
   Find words in the text that mean:
   a. during the day: _____
   b. very rapidly: _____
4. Have the student write out complete sentences based on the text with words on which they need to focus their attention. They shouldn't reproduce the text exactly, but reuse the vocabulary in a different grammatical form (different person, number, tense, etc.).
5. Have the student complete a paragraph or sentence in any way they want using the different choices given:
   Outside, the (flowers, water, street) of the (lake, city, garden) had a/an unpleasant (appearance, color, odor) because it

was contaminated by the (swamps, tourists, cars) that (circulate, walk, flow) through them.

The student should write out the paragraph as a complete version, read it over to see if it makes sense, then share it with you or their group and see what results they come up with. This teaches the student to not only pay attention to distinctions of meaning but also to a comprehension exercise.

6. A variation of #1 above can be to associate an action with an object:
   you can eat it (bread)
   you can look at/pick/plant it (flowers)
   you can read/open/close it (book)
7. Have the student underline, circle, or cross out the word that doesn't belong:
   blue, red, cold, green
   tree, flower, wall, grass
   hot, cold, warm, honor
8. Write out words that have a natural association with a word:
   house: room, kitchen, furniture, window, door, wall
9. Give the student a simple sentence of two or three words and see how many separate words they can make from it.
   es un árbol: es, un, árbol, se, su, sol, lo, los, la, las, no, son, rosa, un, una, unas, luna
10. Choose a word from the current lesson and see how many expressions can be written containing the word (in this example, "time"), and then create a sentence to use it:
    at the same time, another time, time out, from time to times

These are just samples of how you can help a student learn by thinking for themselves. And it gives them more confidence when they can find the right answer to the problem.

▪ THE POWER OF LANGUAGE

Learning Without a Textbook

Textbooks are intended to introduce vocabulary and grammatical constructions in stages. Let us say there is no book available. You can still gather vocabulary from a dictionary and grammar notes from a grammar reference book. You must have access to both; otherwise, you will find it very difficult to teach yourself.

Since these types of books follow a set and formalized pattern for ease of reference, your main job is to find, select, and put into order the material into something like you find in a textbook. This will involve extra work, of course, but you will be able to overcome the problems of learning without a textbook. As we will see later in this book, some reading texts will soon become a required addition to the grammar book and dictionary. Newspapers or magazines (either online or the ones in the shops) would make satisfactory substitutes.

Essential vocabulary

Please note that what follows is not a scheduled plan of procedure. What I am showing here are the most important vocabulary words that form a solid foundation for learning a foreign language. Details on using them are given in *The Speak Up! Language Challenge* language series of books.

Most Commonly Used Verbs

to be	to have
to have	to like
to like	be fond of
be fond of	to do
to do	to make
to make	

Helper Verbs / Infinitives

These verbs are used in situations where one verb just isn't enough. For example, "I'm going to go pay for the meal."

to be called	to hurt
to buy	to like
to cost	to live
to do	to make
to drink	to pay
to eat	to see
to enter	to sleep
to help	

Building Blocks

The following words are the building blocks of a sentence: These are the small words that either complete a sentence or combine two sentences into one.

afterwards	during
all	everything
already	for
also	from
and	good
another	here
bad	in order to
because	in
but	later
(a) little	to, toward
more	too much
much	too
nearby	until
nothing	very
there are	with
there is	

Question Words

how?	when?
how many times?	where?
how many?	which?
how much?	who?
how often?	why?
what?	

Power language construction

The following snippets of statements and questions are a few examples of the power language constructions you'll find in your studies; there will be many more in real-world conversation. In the next chapter, I will be showing you just how you can take any sentence you see in any context and break it down to its basic structure to create hundreds of sentences from just a handful of vocabulary words.

Can you…?
Do you have (a)…?
Here is my…
I am here for…
I am here with…
I have (a)…
I must…[infinitive]
I'm…
Is this…to [placename]?
Is this…?
It is…
May I…here?
May I have…?
May I see…?
May I speak with…?
This is (too)…
What does…cost to [placename]?
What does…cost?
What does it cost per…?
What is…?

When is…going to [placename]?
When is…going?
Where are…?
Where is…?
[object]…does not work.

The Power Chart Method

The quickest way to learn a language is to start using it. To do so, the first thought most people have is to find as much material as possible for speech practice. And I agree—the more you have, the better. But you must be aware of the dangers this can present.

Do not restrict yourself to just a few sentences; memorize them by heart. You will eventually find yourself repeating them like a parrot, and trying to apply what you have learned to new material will prove difficult.

Do not attempt to practice too many different types of sentences that have no relation to each other. This will put a strain on your memory, and your progress will be slowed down.

You can avoid these dangers by creating sentences with a common grammatical structure or pattern, and by changing a word or two, you can change the meaning with little effort.

Let me show you what I mean

How many sentences can you make with the following vocabulary list?

boy	office
girl	park
home	store
is	the
going	to
man	went
not	woman

I'll start you off with one: **The boy is going to the store**. Now, stop and think about how many sentences you can make with the addition of other vocabulary. Instead of "boy," you could use girl, man, or woman, giving you the ability to use four different sentences.

The	**boy** **girl** **man** **woman**	is going to the store

Let's use a few more words. Instead of going to the store, the person could be going to the office, the park, or going home. And with those three words, we just expanded our chart to sixteen sentences.

The	boy girl man woman	is going	to	**the store** **the office** **the park**
				home

Let's take it up a notch. Can the verb element "is going" also be changed? Maybe they already went to their destination, or they did not go there.

The	boy girl man woman	**is going** **is not going** **went**	to	the store the office the park
				home

Did you notice? In just a few minutes, we created a total of forty-eight sentences simply by using fourteen vocabulary elements.

That's the power of language right there. By arranging vocabulary words in a chart form like this, not only are you acquainting yourself with their meanings and spellings, but you are also seeing them as complements of a whole sentence. After all, isn't that what words are intended to be?

How to use the power charts

To use these charts for review and practice, read the first sentence, The boy is going to the store, as many times as you like until you can do so without having to read each word. Then move on to the next word: the boy is going to the school; the boy is going to the office, etc. Once you can do this without difficulty, you can then either switch to the negative form or introduce another subject (the girl, the man). Once you can go through them all successfully, you will have spoken forty-eight full sentences, all grammatically correct. Then construct another pattern with a different example sentence in your lesson and repeat the process.

How different is it from the textbook?

By simply doing the exercises in a textbook the way they would have you do, all you're doing is practicing translation without any flexibility. But if you adopt the Power Chart Method, you will have practiced speaking, reading, writing, interpreting, and translating all at the same time.

Expanding the pattern in selecting material

One of the purposes of arranging sentence patterns into these charts is to increase the number of examples with which to practice. Most textbooks devote half a dozen pages to grammatical theory and then present a little more than half a page of exercises based on all that grammar. If you are given as little as ten sentences to practice, it will seem that too much work would be involved in expanding each one into a power chart. But you will also find that one pattern could cover most sentences given in the lesson material. For example, the Power Chart we built in the previous section was taken from one sentence with eight extra vocabulary words added concerning the subject of that sentence (the boy). This method may easily increase the exercise material, so if you are presented with ten sentences, you can easily increase it to one hundred or more!

Paying attention to grammar

Once you understand the pattern concept, you may find that the change in one element may affect the rest of the sentence. Look at these examples in both English and Spanish. While it is possible to say **La calle es pequeña** (the street is small), **La casa es pequeña** (the house is small), and **La ciudad es pequeña** (the city is small), it is not possible to describe cars the same way: **El auto es pequeño** (the car is small). That's because *pequeña* is the feminine form of the adjective "small," which, in Spanish grammar, nouns, and adjectives must agree as to their endings. Now, the word "car" in Spanish (auto) is a masculine noun and uses an "-o" ending to indicate that, necessitating the change of *pequeña* to *pequeño*.

To further illustrate, let us take the following vocabulary:

la actriz—the actress
grande—big
el chico—the boy
gordo—fat
la niña—the girl
es—is

no es—is not
el hombre—the man
el cartero—the postman
pequeña—small
delgado—thin
la mujer—the woman

And we'll arrange it into a power chart, making sure to create a feminine form of the adjective for each of the feminine nouns. These twelve vocabulary words give you the materials you need to create ninety-six complete sentences.

el cartero el chico el hombre	es no es	delgado gordo grande pequeño
la actriz la niña la mujer		delgada gorda grande pequeña

This chart is a perfect example of the distinction that arises in many sentence patterns, so it is essential to follow the grammar section of a textbook closely and read through the sentences in the exercises before constructing a chart.

Also, it is best to keep in mind that some forms of a verb are not affected by the distinction between masculine and feminine. It will have its own space in the chart, as shown above, to show that it applies to all subjects.

Once you learn the use of masculine and feminine forms of nouns and adjectives, it will increase your conversational fluency to combine two short sentences into one. For example, ***El hombre es viejo y la mujer es vieja*** (the man is old and the woman is old), ***El auto es pequeño y la ciudad es grande*** (the car is small and the city is big), etc.

When it starts getting complicated

As we have seen so far, the languages belonging to the Romance family (Catalan, French, Italian, Latin, Portuguese, Romanian, and Spanish) can be easily converted through the Power Chart method. The next question is, what about those languages with a more complicated grammatical structure, such as the Germanic and Slavic languages?

Let's take a look

The first difficulties for a learner of those languages are indeed not only about gender (masculine, feminine, and neuter), but there are also cases of nouns (nominative, accusative, genitive, dative, etc.). Any of these factors will affect the form of the noun and the form of the article that goes with it. Let me give you an example in German, starting with a vocabulary list:

findet—finds
hört—hears
der Hund—dog
der Mann—man

sieht—sees
der Sohn—son
sucht—looks for
der Vogel—bird

The chart for this list can look like this:

Der	Mann Sohn Hund Vogel	sieht hört sucht findet	den	Mann Sohn Hund Vogel

Notice the word *den*? This is the form of the article *der* in the accusative case—the direct object of the sentence. If you can spend a few minutes practicing with the sixty-four sentences in this chart, it will result in a quick mastery of the nominative and accusative cases of masculine nouns without having to learn the rules and exceptions to the rules.

Speaking of which, a book or language class will put the cases of all three genders of the articles into a table like the one below and tell you to memorize or learn it:

	Masc	**Fem**	**Neut**
Nominative	der	die	das
Accusative	den		

The Speak Up! Method of Language Learning

Now stop and take a moment to look closer at that table. Did you notice that there is no accusative form for feminine or neuter nouns? This cuts down on a lot of your learning time. Instead, all you need to do is construct a pattern that immediately gives you all three genders. Let me show you a few new words to drive it home.

die Frau—woman, wife
die Katze—cat
das Mädchen—girl
das Pferd—horse

Der	Mann / Hund	sieht / hört / sucht / findet	den	Hund / Mann
Die	Frau / Katze		die	Katze / Frau
Das	Mädchen / Pferd		das	Pferd / Mädchen

The Spanish, French, and German sentences we have been looking at in this book so far have been similar in pattern to their English equivalents. Some languages that are related to English will show some differences not used in English. Let's use Swedish for this example.

The Swedish Language

One peculiarity about the Swedish language that affects the feel of the sentence is the use of an enclitic definite article (meaning it is attached to the noun like a suffix). Here is a quick look at an explanation of the articles with a vocabulary list from my Swedish textbook:

Nouns are classified as either common or neuter. The indefinite article (a, an) is either **en** or **ett** according to the gender, and the definite article (the) is formed by suffixing either **-en** or **-ett** to the noun.

		a, an	**the**
Common	horse	en häst	hästen
	girl	en flicka	flickan
	person	en person	personen
Neuter	animal	ett djur	djuret
	mouse	ett möss	mösset
	child	ett barn	barnet

Now that we have this information, let us build a chart from these words as follows:

Hästen Flickan Personen	är	en	person flicka häst
Djuret Mösset Barnet	är inte	ett	barn möss djur

From this chart, you have enough material to painlessly introduce you to the use of both Swedish articles. And here is another advantage to this arrangement: even though all the sentences produced from this chart are grammatically correct, not all of them are going to make sense. And once you notice whether a sentence makes sense or not (*e.g., Flickan är ett djur*), that means you are very aware of the meaning, which is the first step to <u>thinking</u> in the second language. This will also help you later when questions are introduced into the conversation and the above pattern can be used to answer them. Try it and answer the following question: **Är flicken ett djur?**

More unnecessary grammar

Do you recall in the German examples how unnecessary it was to learn the accusative forms of die and das because they were the same as the nominative forms? Similarly, in Swedish, it is not necessary to learn that the article ending *-en* drops the *-e* part if the word ends in a vowel. Look at the vocabulary list again, and you will see where *flicka* becomes *flickan*. This change is automatically incorporated into the pattern and automatically learned through usage.

Languages unrelated to English

Can the Power Chart method also be used with languages that are not related to the Germanic or Romance languages?

Answer: Yes!

Let me use an example with Welsh, where the differences in a sentence pattern would be even more obvious since the verb is placed at the beginning of the sentence.

Mae'r bws yn aros ar y stryd

is a bus stopping in the street.

This example uses the same concept as our example in the beginning: *The boy is going to the store*. With that in mind, let me provide you with twelve more vocabulary words with which you will be able to create about one hundred ninety different sentences!

ar y stryd—in the street   mynd—going
bws—bus   plismon—policeman
car—car   rhedeg—running
cerdded—walking   tad—father
i'r dref—to the town   yn aros—stopping
i'r parc—to the park   yn y sgwar—in the square

	bws	yn aros	ar y	stryd
Mae'r	car	mynd		sgwar
	tad	cerdded		dref
	plismon	rhedeg	i'r	parc

How complicated can it get?

Of course, not all forms of communication will be made up of short, simple sentences. I have a *Teach Yourself Norwegian* book from 1967, and in chapter 14, they give you the following to translate:

- I am to meet my wife at the station, and I don't dare to come too late,
- I wouldn't have gone away if I had known that you were in town.
- It would have been better if you could have come tomorrow.

At first glance, this may look intimidating, so how will you manage to find a way around complicated sentences like those? What you are looking at is a larger amount of words than what we have been working within this book. Look at them again, and you will see that the basic core of the sentence patterns is still there:

- **I am to meet my wife at [the station],** and I don't dare to come too late.
- **I wouldn't have gone away** if I had known that you were in town.
- **It would have been better if** you could have come tomorrow.

As you advance in your lessons, you will develop a feel for each type of sentence, and with a fair amount of vocabulary learned during your lessons, you will find that similar sentences can be made based on the core model of the sentence.

In the real world

In the real world of communication, you are not going to be using simple sentences all the time. You have conversations you read newspapers, magazines, websites, etc., which allows you to see how

The Speak Up! Method of Language Learning

the Power Language method helps you expand your learning capabilities. In a book for learning German, I found this short reading text:

> Wien ist eine sehr schöne Stadt. Es gibt hier alte Kirchen und schöne Museen. Es gibt auch ein großes Opernhaus und viele Theater. Wien ist bekannt für gute Musik und gutes Essen. Ich gehe oft zu Konzerten und höre die wunderschönen Walzer von Johann Strauss. Ich gehe auch ins Theater. Die Theaterstücke sind sehr interessant.

There are five full sentences here that have a similar grammatical pattern, thus allowing us to create some new vocabulary lists and Power Charts. Here are two sentences from that paragraph:
Es gibt hier alte Kirchen und schöne Museen.
Es gibt auch ein großes Opernhaus und viele Theater.
Now let's break them down into a vocabulary list (eliminating any duplicates, of course).

alte—old
auch—also
ein—a, an
die Kirche(n)—church(es)
das Museum—Museum
Opernhaus—opera house
schöne—beautiful

es gibt—there is/there are
großes—big
hier—here
Theater—Theaters
und—and
viele—many

And using what we've learned so far, the following Power Chart is constructed:

Es gibt	hier	hier auch	alte Kirchen ein großes Opernhaus	und	schöne Museen viele Theater

Here are the other three sentences found in the text. Can you create a vocabulary list (including any words from the example above) along with a Power Chart to organize them?

Ich gehe oft zu Konzerten.
Ich höre die wunderschönen Walzer von Johann Strauss.
Ich gehe auch ins Theater.

On the companion website, you'll find some examples of texts from newspaper articles, magazines, and books to give you practice in finding new sentence constructions and making your own collection of Power Charts.

Be sure to find more than one sentence of a particular pattern using the same grammatical point. This will give you more chances of retaining in your memory not just a collection of words but, more importantly, the grammatical structure behind them which will enable you to create many other statements or questions almost on demand.

Question and Answer Method

If you have a language partner, this chapter will prove very useful. And for the student who is learning a language alone, the best way you can get yourself up to conversational speed is to ask yourself questions based on a power chart you made and produce sentences as the answers to those questions. This method may appear difficult and confusing at first, yet after a little bit of practice with a few charts, it can be seen as a better method of learning.

The purpose of language is not to just communicate, but to converse with another human. After all, communication between humans is not just isolated words or small bits of sentences. Rather, it is a series of complete sentences, questions, and answers resulting from questions, forming suppositions and conclusions, expressing opinions, having discussions, etc. If you recall from the section on building Power Charts, you have seen that learning words and phrases built up as complete sentences rather than separate wordlists and grammar explanations makes learning languages a much easier goal to accomplish. I will admit that it does not solve all the problems that language learning may bring up, but it will get you started very quickly and effectively.

Most language courses and classes focus on travel needs. And from what I've experienced over the years, many people traveling to another country for the first time find that they are asking more questions than making statements in conversation—and struggling to do so. This can be somewhat blamed on the indirect method of learning (where the teacher usually asks the questions and the student provides the answers). To fix this problem, make a series of questions and answers based on the materials being learned. This will help you reach a level that results in quicker and more automatic responses, helping you think in a foreign language. It is a practical method since, in most cases, the number of words introducing questions is less than ten.

Who?
What?
What ... like?
Which?
Where?

When?
How?
How much
How many?
Why?

Another advantage of these words is that they will help you learn about other parts of speech in the language you are learning. The words "who?" and "what?" are answered by nouns or pronouns. "Which" is answered by demonstrative words (which door? That one), "when" by adverbs of time, and so on. The question construction "what...like?" is answered by an adjective. In most languages, this is expressed in a less roundabout way:

English: What is her mother like? She is very kind.

French: Comment est sa mère? Elle est très gentille

German: Wie ist ihre Mutter? Sie ist sehr gütig

In addition to the above, many languages have idiomatic expressions that turn a complete sentence into a question that requires a yes-or-no answer. For example, French has *n'est-ce pas?*, German *nicht war?*, Spanish *¿verdad?*, Swedish *eller hur?*, etc. These are similar to

English, *didn't he?*, *aren't you?*, etc. Also, some languages do not have the words for yes or no when used in answers. What they do is repeat the verb, e.g., in Welsh: Did he come? He came. Are you going? I'm not going.

Using power charts

In the early stages, of course, there are very few questions to which sentences from textbook translation exercises lend themselves, but here the main value lies in the constant spoken repetition of similar phrases. Let's take a look at the Swedish Power Chart we built earlier:

Hästen Flickan Personen	är är inte	en	person flicka häst
Djuret Mösset Barnet		ett	barn möss djur

Take a few moments to look over the chart and see if you can create a series of questions and answers like the following:

Q: Är mösset en person?
A: Nej, mösset är inte en person, det är ett djur.

Q: Personen är inte ett djur, eller hur?
A: Nej, det är en person.

Later in your studies when you come upon some reading text, you will discover new ways to ask and answer questions. Here is a paragraph about Bolivia taken from the *Speak Up! In Spanish language course*.

Bolivia está en el centro-oeste de América del Sur. La Bolivia limita al norte y este con

Brasil, al sur con Argentina y Paraguay y al oeste con Chile y el Perú.

Bolivia tiene una superficie de 1.098.581 kilómetros cuadrados y su población es de 10.027.254 de habitantes. Su superficie es la sexta más extensa de Iberoamérica y comprende distintos espacios geográficos.

La capital de Bolivia es Sucre, que tiene una población de 300,000 habitantes. La ciudad se encuentra a una altitud de 2810 metros sobre el nivel del mar.

Taking that text, you can form questions based on the "answers" already provided within the reading itself.

1. ¿Dónde está la Bolivia?
2. ¿Qué país está al norte?
3. ¿Qué país está al sur?
4. ¿Cuál es la capital de Bolivia?
5. ¿Qué población tiene?
6. ¿A qué altitud esta?

Of course, such exercises should already be included with a language course, but when you encounter a paragraph in a newspaper or online, you can use this knowledge to make your own.

An even better challenge would be taking a single word from your vocabulary list and forming questions from it as best you can. For example, the word "baker" in German is **Bäcker**. And the word for "bakery" is **Bäckerei**. So you can ask questions such as:

Was ist ein Bäcker? Ein Mann der Brot macht

Wo arbeitet er? In einer Bäckerei

Practice your writing skills

Using the power chart constructions based on what you've found, write down at least ten complete sentences. They do not have to be too complex. Use simple sentences and avoid too much detail if you are not at that point in your lessons. Stick with what you know, and then check everything that you have written by sharing it with your study group or your language partner, comparing as much material as possible with the original text.

Newspapers and Other Media

So far, I've been talking about the classroom or textbook environment in language learning. Now let's take a quick look at the one area of learning that is seriously overlooked: newspapers, magazines, and online resources.

The best part of learning with these forms of media is the non-ending, continuous text on any topic in which you have an interest. Here you have a live look at the language, allowing you to learn new vocabulary and grammatical constructions "in the wild."

What are the two main goals you should have in mind when using these important learning tools?

1. To meet new grammar constructions and vocabulary and actively learn and practice any new material orally and in writing.
2. To better understand the flow and stylistic usage of the language and increase an intuitive feeling for it, improve your capabilities in thinking in the language.

Active learning

If you have a newspaper or magazine, look for text that is more descriptive rather than narrative. See, what you can find has a straightforward, colloquial style rather than formal, literary stuff.

To help you with your learning, select those articles on subjects with which you are quite well acquainted. You can find this in the smaller articles targeting local news and communities. In this way, you will be able to acquire a larger amount of vocabulary.

New grammar constructions are perfect for creating a new power chart, as outlined in the previous chapter. You can expand on them by using not just already-known vocabulary but also new words taken from the article.

Using the question-and-answer method

This is also a great time to use the question-and-answer method. Select any sentence or two at random and think of them as answers to questions. Can you think of a question that would result in the "answers" you have chosen? Try it with captions in photographs or drawings in the text. Have your language partner ask the meaning of it and give the answer as best you can. This will act as a revision of grammar and vocabulary, all while practicing new material. Record the questions on your phone or tablet, and leaving gaps to repeat the answers. Go over them with your class or language partner in your next study lesson.

Practice your writing skills

Using the power chart constructions based on what you've found in the newspaper and magazine articles, write down at least ten complete sentences. Try writing your captions to any pictures and illustrations that may appear or expand on those already given. Describe what you see in the pictures or drawings. This will help you practice using adjectives and verbs.

Use complete sentences. They do not have to be too complex. Use simple sentences and avoid too much detail if you are not at that point in your lessons. Stick with what you know. Check everything you have written by sharing it with your study group or your language partner, comparing as much material as possible with the original text.

▪ LEARNING WITH ARTIFICIAL INTELLIGENCE

The Impact of AI on Language Learning

It seems that in recent years, artificial intelligence (AI) has been increasingly integrated into various aspects of our digital lives, including language acquisition. The impact of AI on language learning is diverse, providing both opportunities and challenges for educators, learners, and corporate entities. According to a Microsoft survey, many institutions believe that AI will play a key role in improving their competitiveness, securing funding, and promoting innovation.

While AI has its advantages, there are also some drawbacks to consider. Let's consider the pros and cons.

Personalized Learning

AI has the capability to assess an individual's strengths, weaknesses, rate of learning, and preferences to provide a more tailored learning environment. This enhances the learner's involvement in the lesson and maximizes the achievement of learning objectives and goals.

Enhanced and Immediate Feedback

The integration of AI in learning brings about a multitude of benefits, including immediate feedback on pronunciation, grammar, and vocabulary usage. This enables learners to swiftly identify and correct their mistakes, resulting in a more efficient learning process. Real-time analysis provides easily understandable suggestions that can be immediately implemented, eliminating the need for learners to wait for feedback on their progress.

For educators and teachers, AI can be a valuable tool in creating dynamic lesson plans, tracking a student's progress, and pinpointing areas that may need extra attention. This not only enhances the effectiveness of teaching but also lightens some of the workload, thereby reducing the pressure on teachers.

The Downside of Using AI

Lack of human interaction

Language acquisition goes beyond memorizing words and grammar rules; it involves an understanding of cultural nuances and subtle communication cues that AI struggles to grasp. As of the writing of this book (April 25, 2024), AI's effectiveness in certain language settings falls short, especially when providing authentic human interaction when learning a language.

Plagiarism and overreliance

It is important to exercise caution from a legal perspective, as excessive reliance on AI-based tools may impede the development of crucial critical thinking skills necessary for language learners. Overreliance on technology can restrict creativity and the ability to engage in authentic real-life dialogues. Furthermore, educators will need to face the challenge of students turning in AI-generated assignments.

AI-generated content poses a significant challenge in terms of plagiarism. Various antiplagiarism tools, such as SEOTools.com and Turnitin, have integrated features to detect AI-generated content. As a result, a vast number of texts and papers have been identified as AI-generated through these implemented checks, amounting to millions of flagged instances.

Access to resources

Another concern is that equal access to these tools may not be available due to variations in technological advances. Some schools and institutions may have the budgets and resources to invest in AI systems and software, while others may lack the necessary funding to provide even the most basic levels of access for their students.

What does this mean? Students in less privileged communities or schools will miss out on the benefits of AI-powered learning tools and fall behind in their studies. Technology has indeed become cheaper over time, but less privileged communities or institutions will still be using older or previous-generation tech for longer amounts of time until it becomes more affordable.

Privacy and Ethics

Because AI-powered platforms collect a large amount of user data, the issues of data privacy, security breaches, and ethical usage of personal information come up. As AI is implemented more and more in our lives, advanced security systems will need to be implemented and constantly kept up to date to ensure that user data is securely protected from potential data breaches. Similarly, laws will need to constantly develop to keep up to date with these advancements.

The impact of AI on language learning is exciting and historic. Although it offers accessible and efficient learning experiences, there are challenges such as the lack of human interaction and concerns about your data's privacy. It's best to keep and maintain a balanced approach when taking advantage of AI for language education.

ABOUT THE AUTHOR

Since 1978, Sean L. Young has always had a passion for languages. He has studied, learned, and taught over sixty languages and has achieved conversational fluency in half of them. He is the founder of Young's Language Consulting and the creator of *The Rosetta Stone Challenge* and *The Speak Up!* language series. In the 1990s, he was invited to teach in schools and universities in Europe, and later, with the help of the Internet, he expanded his teaching throughout the world. After retiring in 2021, he is now working as an educational consultant, helping to change how languages are taught and learned.

Printed in the USA
CPSIA information can be obtained
at www.ICGtesting.com
CBHW020748261024
16330CB00065B/553